Stoic Game Design

Crafting Immersive Experiences through Wisdom

Table of Contents

Chapter 1. Introduction

Embark on a captivating journey of enlightenment with our Special Report: "Stoic Game Design: Crafting Immersive Experiences through Wisdom". This unique exploration bridges the intriguing worlds of ancient philosophy and modern game design, creating an eloquent symphony of thought-provoking ideas. Who knew that the wisdom of the Stoics could seamlessly blend with contemporary design elements to create immersive, life-altering gaming experiences? Packed with inspiring insights, incisive analyses, and demonstrative case studies, this report isn't simply a collection of words, but a gateway to uncharted dimensions of creativity. The marriage of antiquity and technology has never been more engaging or stimulating. So why wait to unwrap this treasure chest of knowledge? This special report promises not just to educate, but to transform your perspective, setting you on a wisdom-infused voyage of discovery. Create with heart, design with soul, and watch an astonishing universe of Stoic-inspired gaming unfold before your eyes.

Chapter 2. The Symbiosis of Stoicism and Game Design

Many may initially see an incongruity between the ancient philosophy of Stoicism and the modern field of game design. Yet, upon deeper investigation, intriguing parallels emerge. We are embarking now on a fascinating exploration into how applying Stoic concepts can deepen and enrich the process of game design and its resultant creations.

2.1. Stoicism in a Nutshell

Before delving into the symbiotic relationship between Stoicism and game design, it's crucial to understand the core tenets of Stoicism. Stoicism, an ancient Greek philosophy, champions the idea that we cannot control the world around us. We can, however, dictate our reactions to external events. By focusing on what's within our control—our decisions, beliefs, and feelings—we can lead a harmonious life.

It posits life's challenges becoming less daunting if viewed as a part of the natural course of events, rather than disruptive disturbances. With equanimity at its heart, Stoicism encourages individuals to view every setback as an opportunity for growth, to cultivate resilience, and willingly embrace change rather than resisting it.

Now let's look at how these profound principles might infuse and be expressed in the world of game design.

2.2. Embedding Stoic Concepts into Game Mechanics

Video games have long integrated philosophical concepts into their narratives or mechanics, subtly prompting players to question and introspect. Stoicism, too, can be woven into game design in multiple ways. Such implantation can guide players towards the implementation of Stoicism within their lives effortlessly and even unconsciously, providing them with wisdom concealed in the guise of entertainment.

One method is by implementing choices within games that mirror the Stoic emphasis on internal locus of control, compelling players to realize that their in-game outcomes aren't merely outcomes of fate or randomness, but the consequences of their actions and choices—that which is in their control.

Consider a game in which the player experiences an unpreventable disaster, like an earthquake destroying the player's city. The player's choices following said disaster would determine the city's recovery. Through such scenarios, the game subtly underscores the Stoic principle of focusing on our reactions to events, rather than the events themselves.

2.3. Narrative - A Powerful Tool for Stoic Integration

Narrative, another potent method for representing philosophical concepts, can be exploited to articulate Stoicism's ideologies. By creating a protagonist who embodies Stoic virtues, designers can convey Stoic philosophy into a visual, relatable form.

Imagine a protagonist designed with unmistakable Stoic values - resilient, accepting, and equanimous. Their journey, filled with setbacks and trials, portrays them responding with composure and persistently adapting according to their inner guiding principles. By observing and learning from such a character, players are likely to internalize these virtues.

2.4. Case Study: Assassins Creed

A noteworthy demonstration of the marriage between Stoicism and game design is shown in the game, "Assassins Creed." In its narrative and themes, the game's protagonist, Altair, is undeniably Stoic—calm, resilient, and governed by his principles over his emotions. Despite the continual hardship and loss thrown his way, Altair repeatedly demonstrates Stoicism—undeterred and unwavering in his convictions, galvanized by adversity rather than crushed.

Not only does Assassins Creed wreathe its storyline with virtuous protagonists demonstrating stoic resilience, but it also nudges players towards a Stoic outlook themselves. By placing players in situations that challenge their patience, wisdom, and resilience, it reinforces Stoic values like resilience, empathy, and equanimity within players.

2.5. Reinterpretation of Stoic Virtues in Game Design

Let's now discuss the reinterpretation of Stoic virtues within game design. The four cardinal virtues of Stoics are wisdom, courage, justice, and temperance. These virtues can be employed creatively in the conceptualization of game goals, conflict, mechanics, and dynamics.

For instance, the conceptualization of these virtues as "skills" that a player needs to develop to progress through the game. Certain game scenarios could require the player to exhibit temperance and patience, while others may require courage and decisiveness. This not only links back to the Stoic perception of life as a perpetual training ground for virtues but also adds layers of complexity to game design.

2.6. Limits and Constraints - The Stoic Designer's Perspective

Game design isn't merely about crafting immersive player experiences—it's about crafting those experiences within certain constraints. Budget, time, and technical limitations not infrequently challenge a designer's creativity and resilience.

This is where the stoic designers can showcase their true mettle. Embracing these limitations, per the Stoic belief, the game designers can see these constraints not as obstacles but as opportunities. Necessity, they say, is the mother of invention, and these restrictions could pave the way for novel ideas and unanticipated masterpieces.

2.7. Conclusion

By effectively bridging the gap between Stoicism and game design, we open the doors to a unique realm where philosophy cohabitates seamlessly with technology. With patience, equanimity, and wise judgement as their allies, game designers can not only create more profound, enriching gaming experiences but also foster personal growth in their players, thereby making game design a conduit of wisdom. It becomes imbued with soul, transforms into practical philosophy—an engaging, interactive method of spreading vital life insights packaged within enjoyable digital environments. This is the potential offered through the symbiosis of Stoicism and game design.

Chapter 3. Stoic Philosophy: A Brief Introduction for Game Developers

Ancient wisdom and modern technology may seem odd bedfellows, but as we delve beneath the surface, their complex symphony unravels. Even before delving into programming, game mechanics, or aesthetics, a fundamental understanding of the philosophy you're trying to parlay into your creations will act as the guiding north star. The profound teachings of Stoic philosophy could prove transformative for game design, weaving valuable life lessons into virtual landscapes and plots.

3.1. The Foundations of Stoicism

Stoicism was born in the bustling city of Athens in 3rd century BC within the mind of Zeno of Citium. He, along with his successors Cleanthes and Chrysippus, formulated and expanded a philosophy focused on clear perception, rationality, personal responsibility, and disciplined actions. Stoic teachings urged individuals to focus only on the elements within their control—thoughts, actions, reactions—and accept the rest with serenity and unaltered tranquility.

3.2. Stoic Philosophy: Key Concepts for Game Developers

Stoicism is built on several pivotal concepts that could effectively inspire game development, forming the backbone of immersive and influential gaming experiences.

1. *The Dichotomy of Control:* Stoics affirm control only over their

actions, reactions, and judgements. Elements beyond their control are accepted as indifferent, and this outlook fosters a calm acceptance of life's vicissitudes. In the context of game design, this can give rise to game mechanics or narratives that explore these dynamics, pushing players to discern their locus of control and adapt strategies accordingly.

2. *Virtue is the Sole Good:* Stoics perceive virtue — prudence, courage, justice, and temperance — as the only true good. Virtue, for them, is a disciplined expression of the rational part of the soul and the path to eudaimonia or a fulfilled life. This emphasis on virtues can be woven into game characters, challenges, and rewards systems, steering players toward making virtuous choices.

3. *Understanding Nature:* Stoicism encourages aligning oneself with Nature. The Stoics perceived the universe as a rational and interconnected entity. Games can encourage players to understand and respect their environment, whether that's the physical game world, the rules of the system, or interacting with other characters or players.

3.3. Stoicism and Game Narratives

Stoic principles find resonating echoes in popular game narratives. From seasoned adventurers embodying stoic virtues to quests that touch upon the dichotomy of control, Stoicism's fingerprints are subtly discernible in multiple game narratives.

Games like 'The Legend of Zelda: Breath of the Wild' and 'Dark Souls' serve as notable examples. They exemplify a harmonious blend of stoic principles and gaming elements, pushing the player to face hardships bravely, understand their game environment (nature), make rational decisions, and master control over their emotions and actions.

3.4. Stoicism and Game Mechanics

Applying stoic philosophy to game mechanics could profoundly shape the player's experience and learning journey. For instance, a game introducing mechanics stressing on the dichotomy of control could effectively teach players wisdom in delineation. Designing gaming situations that are beyond the player's control and others where they have full autonomy enforces this stoic concept.

Furthermore, embracing stoicism in game reward systems can be powerful. Creating rewards tied to showcasing stoic virtues and rational choices can redefine the in-game experience. Aligning in-game accomplishments with these virtues transcends the virtual environment, potentially influencing players' real-world outlooks.

3.5. Stoicism, Game Design, and Emotional Mastery

The fusing of Stoicism with game design elements can result in a unique breed of games — games that cater not just to the thrill of winning but also lessons in emotional handling, resilience building, and wisdom acquisition. More importantly, these games would provide a safe virtual space where players can encounter powerful emotions, understand them, alter their responses, and strive for emotional mastery—reflecting the very crux of stoic teachings.

Stoicism, when viewed closely, seems tailor-made for adaptation into the gaming realm. Its percepts of virtue driving fulfilment, acceptance of what's beyond control, and the disciplined pursuit of wisdom serve as goldmines for game narratives, mechanics, and player character development. Infusing games with its wisdom and practical insights presents a unique opportunity to elevate not just the gaming experience, but potentially, the lives of those who play. It's time to craft games that do more than simply entertain — games that illuminate, inspire, and transform.

Chapter 4. Cultivating Wisdom - The Heart of Stoicism and Game Design

Understanding the intricate connection between Stoicism and game design requires that we first delve deeply into the kernel of Stoicism: Wisdom.

At its core, Stoicism places wisdom on high as the ultimate virtue, the pinnacle of human understanding and capability. It's a foundation upon which we can develop crucial philosophies and shape decisions - a more profound way of living that informs our every action. And this in turn harmonizes beautifully with the fundamental aspects of game design: every decision is informed by a purpose. Every action has a consequence.

4.1. Stoic Philosophy and the Core Tenets

Stoicism, a school of Hellenistic philosophy founded by Zeno of Citium in Athens in the early 3rd century BC, teaches the development of self-control and fortitude to overcome destructive emotions. But how did this ancient philosophy value wisdom so much? We see this in the four cardinal virtues of Stoicism: Wisdom (sophia), Courage (andreia), Justice (dikaiosyne), and Temperance (sophrosyne). Wisdom is considered the governing virtue, the virtue from which all others flow.

Wisdom in Stoicism is the ability to distinguish good from evil. Things like wealth, reputation, and health have no value in themselves; it's our perceptions of these things that give them value. Wisdom allows us to see things as they are, without the illusion or imposture of false beliefs. Virtue is the sole good in Stoicism, and wisdom is what allows us to recognize and practice it.

4.2. The Intersection of Stoicism and Game Design

In game design, the creation and development process demands a form of wisdom in its own right. Game designers stand at the crossroads of technical proficiency and creative artistry, crafting worlds, characters, and narratives that not only entertain players but often challenge their perspectives and engage their critical thinking skills.

Much in the same way that Stoicism encourages wisdom through comprehension of one's perceptions, game design drives understanding through mechanics, systems, and narrative. Games function as complex, moving parts of a larger machine - and the best designers understand how these parts interact and influence each other.

When we design with wisdom at the forefront, we create games that go beyond mere entertainment. These are games that invoke thoughtful self-reflection and challenge players to question their perceptions, much in the way that Stoic philosophy urges us to challenge our conceptions of the world around us.

4.3. Case Study: That Dragon, Cancer

To understand the manifestation of Stoic wisdom in game design, let's turn our attention to one extraordinary example: That Dragon, Cancer. The game, a uniquely poignant exploration of pain, loss, and the hope that can emerge even from the darkest moments, acts as an embodiment of wisdom-infused design.

In this hauntingly beautiful indie game, players step into the shoes of a father caring for his son who is battling cancer. With its stream-of-consciousness narrative, surrealistic art style, and emotionally charged ambiance, the game offers a rich tapestry of experiences that touch on some of the most profound human emotions. It's an embodiment of wisdom in game design because it doesn't shy away from the difficult aspects of life. Instead, it embraces them.

The genius of That Dragon, Cancer lies in how it uses game design to directly engage the player's empathy and challenge their perceptions of disease, mortality, and love. Through its raw confrontation with the devastating reality of a child's terminal illness, it leads the player on a journey that's heartrending yet illuminating, a journey where pain becomes a lens through which we view life's fleeting beauty.

This showcase of wisdom—the ability to perceive, understand, and accept the unfathomable complexities of life through a game—is what makes That Dragon, Cancer a compelling example of Stoic-infused game design.

4.4. Wisdom Through Mechanics

On a more practical level, the implementation of wisdom can be seen in the very mechanics of game design. In games like chess or Go, wisdom is necessary for the player to make moves that have far-reaching implications, to strategize and predict the consequences of their actions.

Success in these games demands more than simply understanding rules; it's about perceiving patterns, predicting opponent's moves, and making strategy adjustments. This act of foresight and strategic calculation is a form of wisdom, the kind upheld by Stoicism where one learns to see reality for what it is and take actions based on rational understanding.

4.5. Wisdom in Dialogue and Decision Making Systems

Role-playing games (RPGs) are an especially rich ground when it comes to integrating stoic wisdom into game design. Often, these games require players making decisions that could influence the world's balance, challenging their moral compass and strategic thinking.

In "The Witcher" series, for example, players need to make incredibly nuanced decisions, with each choice having complex implications. Through stoic wisdom, the game's design pushes players to contemplate their decisions, reflecting on the game's narrative and the potential ripple effects of their choices. This intentional design invokes a form of wisdom, a stoic-like introspection that often goes beyond the game and into the player's reality.

4.6. The Journey Forward

As we've explored, wisdom forms the thematic marrow of Stoicism and the philosophical underpinning of well-crafted game design. Not only does it inform design decisions, but it also bridges the gap between creator and player, facilitating meaningful engagement and profound experiences.

Incorporating wisdom in game design isn't just about the practical aspects of game mechanics. It's a holistic approach that encompasses aesthetics, narrative, mechanics, and the player's journey itself. As such, the cultivation of wisdom – acknowledging the power of embracing virtues and understanding consequences – becomes paramount not only in creating deeply immersive gaming experiences but also in engaging players in a transformative way.

We embark on this journey, merging antiquity and technology, philosophy and game design, to better express the human condition.

As we traverse this path, we do more than just create; we inspire, connect, and enrich the gaming community, carrying the torch of wisdom forward across a new frontier. And in doing so, we echo the stoics; we achieve wisdom not as an end unto itself, but as a continuous journey.

Chapter 5. The Stoic Game Designer: Applying Ancient Principles to Modern Challenges

The intriguing exploration of stoic principles often begins within the confines of the ancient world, taking eager knowledge seekers back to starlit courtyards and vast libraries of antiquity. Here, words of wisdom resonated through every echo. The words may be old, but the wisdom — insight into the human condition, advice for maintaining equilibrium in every challenge — is as fresh as an untouched canvas. This wisdom waits to be discovered by the new generation of game designers. But how can we apply this seemingly unrelated body of knowledge to the distinct challenges of game design? The answer lies within the very essence of Stoicism and its astonishing relevance to our modern world.

5.1. 'Know Thyself': A Foundation for Game Design

The Delphic maxim, "know thyself," which is firmly rooted in Stoic philosophy, is a fundamental piece of advice for game designers looking to create deeply impactful experiences. The first step to creating an immersive world lies in understanding one's unique perspective and strengths. A designer's true potential unfolds when reflecting upon their personal experiences, virtues, biases, and inclinations. This introspection forms a baseline for crafting narratives and mechanics that resonate with players on a profound level.

For a game designer, the principle of 'know thyself' can have very practical implications. Analysis of one's strengths may lead a designer to create intricate puzzle-based games if their critical thinking is honed. Alternatively, a designer with strong narrative skills may opt for storytelling-focused adventures. Stoic philosophy encourages us to be genuine with ourselves to understand our true nature, a principle that can help shape the games of tomorrow.

5.2. Mastering Emotional Resilience: An Asset of the Stoic Designer

Game design is a uniquely challenging field. Success is not guaranteed, trial and error is inevitable, and public reception can often feel like a rogue wave in a stormy sea. Faced with these formidable challenges, the stoic principle of emotional resilience becomes an integral part of a game designer's tool kit.

Stoics teach acceptance of elements outside our control. This teaching provides game designers a profound source of strength, resilience, and courage. This philosophy directly translates into better decision-making under stress, helping designers learn from failures rather than becoming disheartened. Reactive sentiments are transformed into proactive responses that can shape a game designer's creations into engaging and enduring works.

5.3. Virtue - The Heart of Stoicism and Game Design

For Stoics, virtue is the highest good. This concept of virtue can be translated into game design in multiple dimensions — from ethical game mechanics to creating a gaming environment that promotes virtue among players.

Ethical game mechanics can be designed in a way that rewards virtuous behavior. This might include rewards for teamwork, patience, honesty, or creativity — prominent virtues celebrated by the stoics. Such a game dynamic not only creates a positive gaming environment but also often leads to a more engaged and loyal game community.

A game that promotes virtue may also entail designing experiences that illuminate the consequences of vice. Game narratives can encompass lessons about conceited ambition, unchecked wrath, or unmitigated duplicity. Such games stand out from the crowd, not just for their entertaining content, but also their message.

5.4. The Dichotomy of Control: Creating Balance

The Stoic principle of the dichotomy of control states that we should focus our energy on what we can control and accept that which we cannot. For game designers, this philosophy offers a unique perspective on balancing player autonomy and narrative progression.

A game that offers no player control becomes a linear narrative, while a game with complete freedom may lose coherence and immersion. Wise application of the dichotomy of control principle can help design a game that maintains an engaging narrative while still giving the player meaningful autonomy.

5.5. Stoicism in Mechanics: An Emphasis on Difficulty and Resilience

Stoics place high importance on resilience in the face of adversity. Accordingly, our game design should involve a satisfying level of challenge to enhance the player's sense of achievement.

Difficulty makes the player's journey meaningful, and through overcoming challenges, players can experience growth within and outside of the game. It is the concept of resilience that fuels 'the hero's journey'—a narrative repeated in many successful game titles, each iteration a testament to the enduring appeal of growth and achievement.

5.6. Connection with Nature: Stoicism in Environmental Design

Stoics emphasized harmony with one's environment. For game designers, utilizing stoic philosophy can help in inspiring exquisite environmental design. Worlds that echo the stark wilderness, peaceful vistas, and the bustling charm of civilization all impart a sense of immersion. The intricate details of a game world can echo the stoic belief in unity and coexistence with the natural world.

These principles offer a glimpse into the expansive universe where Stoicism and game design convene. As designers, it's our challenge to interweave these threads of ancient wisdom into a tapestry of engaging, immersive experiences. The journey may be complex and full of trials, but as the Stoics teach us, it's the journey—and the wisdom gained from it—that makes life meaningful. Through mastering these principles, game designers can transform not just their professional designs, but their personal lives as well.

Chapter 6. Storytelling and the Stoic Craft: Designing Meaningful Experiences

The role of storytelling in game design is as foundational as the structure of a great building. It sets the scene, creates the ambience, and stirs emotions. It provides the raison d'etre for player engagement. However, the implementation of storytelling in game design is often lacking a deeper substance. It is here that the merging of ancient Stoic wisdom brings about a new paradigm – creating a vessel for personal growth through interaction with an immersive, virtual environment.

6.1. The Virtues of Stoic Philosophy

Stoic philosophy presents four cardinal virtues: wisdom, courage, justice, and temperance. These virtues serve as viable, evocative, and emotionally resonating elements when woven into the fabric of the game narrative. By grounding the story in these core virtues, designers can create experiences that not only entertain, but provide players opportunities for introspection and self-knowledge.

Consider how the virtue of wisdom can elevate a game narrative. A character that portrays wisdom doesn't deal with changing circumstances with confusion, but with insight and understanding. He/she is unaffected by the ephemeral world, wielding knowledge as a bridge to the true essence of things. Encountering such characters within a game environment opens up paths of wisdom for players as well.

6.2. Courage as a Game Element

Courage is not about the absence of fear in Stoic philosophy, but the understanding and acceptance of fear. In game design, challenges, enemies, and setbacks can all be tools of manifesting courage. A player's avatar, when confronted with perilous situations, doesn't shy away but faces them bravely. This translates directly into how players perceive threats and confront their fears in real life, setting the game as a practice ground for demonstrating courage.

6.3. Just Characters, Just Games

Justice, a cornerstone of Stoic philosophy, can become a key element within a game narrative, honing the player's ethical compass. Characters that weigh the impact of their actions on others, and adjust to serve fairness, cultivate a sense of justice in the player. Game levels and quests can provide moral dilemmas that require thoughtful decision-making. The consequence system can be designed to reflect the balance of justice directly, rewarding righteous actions and penalising unjust ones.

6.4. Crafting Temperance in Game Design

Temperance, the practice of moderation, is another virtue essential to Stoic teachings. Designing game scenarios that require restraint and measured responses encourages temperance. Scenarios might include limited resources or a stealth mission in which unnecessary actions could lead to failure. Incorporating temperance in the game design invites players to practice control and manage their actions thoughtfully.

6.5. The Stoic Narrative: Memento Mori

One of the most potent Stoic principles to incorporate in game design is 'Memento Mori' - remember that you must die. This concept isn't about fostering fear but prompting the player to ponder on the fleeting nature of life and the importance of making every moment count. Interactive components like timed missions and consequential decision-making systems can underline this principle effectively, instilling a sense of urgency and Zen-like focus on the present moment.

6.6. Applying Dichotomy of Control

Another powerful Stoic concept is the Dichotomy of Control, the understanding that some things are within our control and others are not. This principle can form the basis of the conflict or challenge in the narrative design. For example, players might strive to control their character's mental state through gameplay choices, while external game events remain unaffected by their actions – just as in real life.

6.7. Player Engagement through Stoic Challenges

The essence of Stoic philosophy is not in pure knowledge but its application in life's challenges. Accordingly, game designers can create Stoic missions - objectives based around realising and employing Stoic principles. This not only deepens engagement but provides a means to synthesize philosophical knowledge into practical wisdom.

6.8. A Stoic Ending

Game narratives have a profound potential to leave lasting impressions on a player's mind. This influence lends an excellent opportunity to utilize the concept of preferred indifferents from Stoic philosophy – promoting the idea of peace and contentment in accepting things as they are. Closing the narrative on a Stoic note can transport the player towards newfound perceptions, unravelling a transformative gaming experience.

Stoic storytelling in game design isn't merely about replicating the Stoic principles, but about embedding them within the game mechanics, dynamics, and aesthetics. It offers an engaging, immersive, wisdom-infused voyage, guiding players towards self-awareness and philosophical enrichment at every turn.

Chapter 7. From Pixels to Virtues: Ethical Implications of Stoic Game Designs

Consider a pixel. It's a straightforward light-emitting square, an uncomplicated unit of digital visual information. However, when countless pixels come together, crafted with purpose and intention, they can become an immersive, interactive universe. This chapter explores how such digital realms can serve as platforms for imparting Stoic wisdom, and how that wisdom can inform ethical decision-making within game design.

7.1. Stoicism: A Glance at Ancient Wisdom

Stoicism, a philosophy conceived by Zeno of Citium in the early 3rd century BC, has survived tumultuous eras, war-stricken landscapes, and the caprices of time. Far from being a mere philosophical doctrine, Stoicism is a practical life guide. It teaches acceptance of facts as they are, encourages virtuous behaviour, and advocates for tranquility as a fundamental life purpose. The Stoic philosophers understood that the only thing truly under our control is our own mind, and therein lies our ultimate freedom.

7.2. Stoicism In Game Design

The burgeoning field of game design, at its core, is about crafting interactive experiences. But what if these experiences could serve a higher purpose? What if, amongst quests, rewards, and world-building, game designers could inject valuable lessons of Stoic philosophy?

The concept isn't simply about educating the player; it's about aligning the gameplay mechanics, narrative arc, and player's experience with Stoic principles. The challenge is to embed these principles so seamlessly that players are engrossed in the game world, yet subtly guided towards virtues of wisdom, courage, justice, and temperance – the four cardinal virtues of Stoicism.

7.3. Wisdom: Gameplay Mechanics and Decision making

In the realm of Stoicism, wisdom is often associated with discernment, essential for decision-making. Game designers can utilize this construct by integrating choices that demand a player's discernment. Games that provoke players to make choices based on understanding, rather than impulse, subtly invoke the Stoic wisdom principle.

7.4. Courage: Narrative Arc and Challenges

The virtue of courage, according to the Stoics, does not merely translate to physical bravery. It also encompasses moral courage – standing up for what one believes in and making right yet difficult choices. Game narratives that demand moral courage, where players must overcome obstacles that test their resilience or ethical fibers, offer an immersive way to express this Stoic principle.

7.5. Justice: Social Dynamics within the Game

Justice, in Stoicism, refers to honesty, fairness, and morally right behavior. In multi-player games, or games with AI-controlled characters, designers can foster an environment of justice. In-game consequences corresponding to a player's integrity, honesty, and fairness can translate to an experiential learning of the importance of justice, as viewed by Stoicism.

7.6. Temperance: Feedback and Game Balance

Temperance, under Stoic philosophy, suggests moderation and self-control. In game design, a feedback system that rewards balance and discourages excess can be a subtle transmission medium for this principle. It may be simple as in-game resources management, requiring measured and temperate usage.

7.7. Ethical Implications of Stoic Game Designs

Creating a game implicitly signifies designing an experience, scripting behaviors, and governing motivations, all of which bring ethical considerations to the forefront. In the context of Stoic game design, this involves more than just "fair play" rules or consequences for in-game transgressions. The marriage of Stoicism with game design encourages designers to think about the ethical implications of the worlds they create. It asserts that acknowledging the tremendous influence games have in shaping perspectives, it is crucial to use this power responsibly, cultivating a design ecosystem that promotes empathy, respect, and humanity.

Let us observe how virtue-oriented game design could invite ethical dilemmas. Suppose a player is compelled to make a choice, each option consistent with one Stoic virtue but conflicting with another. Situations where no course of action appears entirely virtuous can initiate internal conflict within players, prompting them to delve deeper into their ethical understanding.

7.8. Unconscious Learning - The Power Of Stoic Game Design

Where a traditional approach to teaching Stoic philosophy might incorporate textbooks and lectures, a game designed with Stoic principles can offer an immersive, interactive, and enjoyable method of learning. Players who engage in Stoic-inspired games don't just read about ancient virtues - they experience them firsthand, navigating simulated scenarios that encourage them to embody these principles.

In conclusion, Stoicism and game design, despite originating from vastly different eras and disciplines, can come together fruitfully. When pixels merge to form not just visually stunning territories, but also experiences steeped in timeless wisdom, we transition from game design to virtue design. It is this potential that makes exploring the interplay between Stoicism and game design both exciting and essential, taking us one step closer to nurturing a more empathetic and ethically cognizant digital generation.

Chapter 8. The Stoic Sandbox: Crafting Player Experiences and Freedom

The concept of a Sandbox game is inherently Stoic in nature. It frames the world as a place where the player can act, but does not necessarily control the outcome of those actions. This cognitive process aligns closely with the Stoic advice to focus on what you can control and accept what you can't. But let us dive in deeper into what this entails for the game designer.

8.1. Stoicism: A Primer

Before embarking on translating Stoic principles into the domain of game design, let's clarify what we mean by Stoicism. Stoicism is an ancient Greek philosophy that encourages individuals to find peace by focusing on what is within their control - usually their thoughts, judgments, and actions - and accepting what is not.

The philosophy encourages a mindful way of life that strives for inner tranquility. Whatever life throws at you, good or bad, it advises viewing it with equanimity. It has surprisingly modern appeal, offering practical advice for cultivating resilience, tranquillity, and wisdom in a turbulent world.

8.2. The Sandbox: A Broad Canvas

The beauty of Sandbox games lies in their inherently immersion-optimized design. Unlike a linear narrative, Sandbox games grant players the freedom to purse their in-game objectives in a manner they find engaging. This player agency is empowering and is the perfect backdrop for incorporating Stoic principles that will subtly guide players towards the path of wisdom.

It's important to understand that as designers, our job isn't to force philosophical musings on the players. Instead, we have to thoughtfully craft a playground where these exquisite pearls of Stoic wisdom can be found.

8.3. The Stoic Game Engine: Cause and Effect

One of the elementary principles of Stoicism is understanding the dichotomy of control - distinguishing the things you can change from those you can't, and focusing your efforts on the former. In a Sandbox game, mastering this principle allows the players' territory to stretch from 'reactive' to 'proactive'.

In action, this involves the careful design of cause and effect scenarios. For instance, the player might be responsible for cueing an event - this could involve building a haven for wanderers, influencing the development of a city or causing its downfall. The 'effect' part is out of players' control - they can't necessarily dictate who will visit the haven, or how the city's residents will react to their actions. In other words, the game should grant players the autonomy to act, but not to control the outcomes of those actions.

8.4. Challenges and Losses: Opportunity for Growth

The Stoics viewed challenges as opportunities for personal growth. By presenting difficult situations, hardship, or even failure, developers can encourage growth and resilience in players. This doesn't necessarily translate into increasingly difficult stages or killing off characters but can also mean decision-making under pressure, resolving conflicts without violence, or dealing with the consequences of their actions.

8.5. Social Relationships: Reflections of Stoic Ideals

A bedrock of Stoic thinking underlines the power of virtuous social relationships. Nourishing these connections in a gaming context can be remarkably transformative. For instance, players can be given the task to navigate complex relationships with their game characters - some relationships might bring joy, others, sadness or even anger. The unpredictability of these interactions mirrors real-life scenarios, reinforcing the value of a poised, Stoic response in the face of varying emotions.

8.6. Closing Realm: Embedding the Stoic Wisdom

Designers should continuously seek ways to reinforce the Stoic principles throughout the game. This could be through in-game texts, narrative arcs, or character development. As the players travel through the expansive Sandbox, they should encounter Stoic wisdom naturally, enhancing their gaming experience and personal growth.

In conclusion, crafting a Stoic Sandbox game is a creative and contemplative process. The aim should not be to interweave profound philosophical teachings in the fabric of the game, but to focus on experiences that embody the wisdom and resilience promoted by Stoicism. Players should exit the game with enriched perspectives, creating memorable experiences both within the gaming universe and in their tangible existence.

Chapter 9. Stoicism and Player Engagement: A Design Perspective

Stoicism, a rich philosophy founded in the Hellenistic period, unravels a plethora of wisdom that can be adeptly harnessed in game design. Encompassing concepts such as resilience, control, and acceptance of the inevitable, Stoicism is a potent tool in creating immersive games. This chapter delves deep into the fascinating conjunction of Stoicism and player engagement from a design perspective.

9.1. Embracing the Dichotomy of Control

At the heart of Stoic philosophy lies the Dichotomy of Control, which stipulates that some things are within our control while others aren't. By integrating this principle in game design, we can provide players with multifaceted experiences, thus enhancing engagement.

Consider a game scenario where players may control their character's actions but have no influence on the overarching game world events. This closely mirrors Stoic teaching: focusing on personal effort and decision-making rather than external factors beyond one's control. Emphasizing on what the player can change – skills, strategies, choices – with the in-game outcomes being secondary, cultivates a sense of responsibility and engagement.

9.2. Resilience and Learning Curves

Endurance is a pivotal Stoic virtue. In game design, resilience can be promoted by curating a skillful blend of challenges and rewards. Reward mechanics should encourage players to persevere, fostering patience and determination. Strategic difficulty spikes and game progression should serve as "teachable moments," mirroring the Stoic lessons of enduring hardships for personal growth.

Think of a game with robust enemy AI, dynamic environments, or challenging puzzles. Instead of explicitly providing solutions, subtle cues or hints nudge players toward the possible strategies. By weathering these trials with resilience, players internalize a valuable life lesson of Stoic philosophy – growth resides not in the avoidance of difficulties, but in their mastery.

9.3. Balancing Virtues and Vices

In Stoicism, virtues are moral gears that aid in navigating life's adversities, while vices impede the journey. In the gaming universe, introducing moral choices can create dynamic narratives, deepening player involvement. Decisions could impact character development, relationships, or the wider game world.

Imagine an RPG where players have to navigate a complex moral landscape that resonates with Stoic morality. Choices are not labeled as 'good' or 'evil,' but are nuanced, incorporating Stoic virtues such as wisdom, courage, justice, and temperance. The ramified storyline, coupled with the in-depth morality system, enhances immersion and engagement.

9.4. Acceptance and Adaptability: Surmounting Frustration

Stoicism urges acceptance of what we cannot change. In game design, infusing elements of randomness, unpredictability, or failure can stir intense emotions. Rather than frustrating players, these elements become fascinating twists driving them to adapt, just as Stoic philosophy advises acceptance and adaptation to life's unpredictability.

Take the example of rogue-like games. They embody the principle of acceptance by featuring permadeath or procedural generation. Accepting the game's volatility and adapting gameplay strategy according to varying circumstances results in potentially infinite player engagement.

9.5. The Perspective of Amor Fati

'Amor Fati' translates to 'love of fate.' The Stoics believed that welcoming whatever happens, even adversity, is the path to peace. In game design, the implementation of this concept could be a game-changer in interactivity and emotional depth, potentially leading to a novel gaming experience.

Anticipate a game with tightly interwoven narrative and gameplay where the players' actions affect not only the in-game characters but the course of the entire game world. Here, embracing 'Amor Fati' isn't a passive acceptance of fate but a dynamic interaction with the game's narrative, engendering profound player engagement.

9.6. Conclusion: The Grand Tapestry of Game Design and Stoicism

Altogether, the implementation of Stoic principles within game design is a transformative process – for both the creator and player alike. As designers, we can use Stoic wisdom to cultivate a more engaging, more enriching gaming experience. By respecting player autonomy, encouraging resilience, providing thought-provoking choices, promoting acceptance, and applauding adaptability, we breathe life into the art of immersive game design. Thus, infusing the age-old wisdom of Stoicism into the algorithms powering modern game experiences can invigorate widespread engagement, deep comprehension, and lasting resonance.

Chapter 10. Case Studies: Successful Implementation of Stoic Principles in Game Design

In exploring the application of Stoic philosophy in game design, it's essential to highlight cases where these principles have been successfully integrated. In each instance, designers have interpreted Stoic concepts and woven them seamlessly into the narrative, mechanics, and aesthetic of various gaming experiences.

10.1. Journey: Embracing the Unchangeable

Placed within a vast desert landscape, Journey is a console-based adventure game where the player navigates through the world, encountering various challenges and undertaking epic quests. There is no dialogue; communication occurs through musical chimes, creating an intricate, wordless interplay among players who cross paths during their journey.

Throughout the game, players are introduced to various elements they cannot control. Weather conditions intensify randomly, and other players enter or exit without warning – all mirroring situations in real life where we encounter unexpected or uncontrollable circumstances. By facing these circumstances bravely and with serenity, the game conveys a potent Stoic message: It is not events themselves that disturb us but rather our interpretation of them.

In the face of hardship, Journey advocates for acceptance and adaptation, leveraging challenges as instruments of personal growth.

As players progress, they learn the power of stoicism in achieving their goals, subtly applying philosophical concepts to their strategies.

10.2. Dark Souls: Understanding the Nature of Challenges and Resilience

Dark Souls takes a relentlessly Stoic approach, immediately plunging players into an unyieldingly harsh world. Players explore a brutal, Gothic-inspired universe, their actions dictated by the game's relentless difficulty.

Due to Dark Souls' notorious challenge level, players must confront failure repeatedly - a staunch representation of the Stoic principle of understanding and embracing hardship as a part of life. The game does not punish death but instead uses every defeat as an opportunity for learning and growth, perfectly embodying the concept of Amor Fati (love of fate). The unpredictability and constant struggle align with the Stoic view of life: events are neither good nor bad; our perception determines their impact.

10.3. The Legend of Zelda: Breath of the Wild: Virtue and Freedom

Breath of the Wild exemplifies another key Stoic principle: freedom through understanding nature (or Physis) and judging only what is within one's control. The player's character, Link, is assigned the task of saving Princess Zelda and, in turn, their world plagued by evil forces. Players have immense freedom to approach this mission, with the ability to explore vast open-world landscapes, discover various tools and weapons, and interact with numerous characters and creatures.

Link's actions are dictated by the player's virtues and understanding of the game's nature. It is this exploration of virtue - courage, wisdom, justice, and temperance - that forms the core of the gameplay, resonating with a critical teaching of Stoicism: virtue is the only true good and vice the only true evil.

10.4. Minecraft: Acceptance and Tranquility

Stoicism isn't just about weathering storms; it's also about finding tranquility and acceptance in simplicity. Minecraft, renowned for its sandbox-style gameplay that encourages construction and creativity, manages to encapsulate this aspect of Stoic thought brilliantly.

A significant portion of the gameplay is just surviving, requiring the player to gather resources, food, and shelter to survive the night. The harsh realities of Minecraft's survival mode imitate real-life situations, prompting players to accept, work with, and react to things beyond their control.

By presenting obstacles that cannot be eliminated but rather endured, Minecraft educates its players about the Stoic principle of Endurance (hypomone), turning a simple game mechanic into a lesson on tranquility and acceptance.

10.5. Conclusion and Future Perspectives

The games we've examined have incorporated Stoic principles into their design in various creative ways, contributing significantly to their players' experiences. By using philosophy not as a backdrop or aesthetic but as a framework for the gameplay itself, designers can offer much deeper, more engaging experiences.

Embracing Stoicism in game design opens a multitude of opportunities: It allows for profound storytelling and innovative gameplay mechanics, delivering a unique experience that expands beyond entertainment—bringing a whole new practical dimension to philosophical teachings. This methodology of making philosophical concepts accessible through gaming has great potential and will be interesting to see how it's leveraged in future game development.

Chapter 11. The Future of Stoic Game Design: Prospects and Challenges

The exploration of Stoicism in game design opens up vast avenues of creativity, novel designs, and immersive gaming experiences. However, predicting its course with precision in the future remains a constructive challenge for game designers and scholars alike. By engaging with key areas of current developments in this direction and investigating challenges that lie ahead, one can frame a surface level path for the evolution of Stoic game design.

11.1. The Role of Stoicism in Narrative Game Design

Stoicism, as a philosophical tool, can profoundly influence the narrative of a game. By integrating the principles of stoicism into the core structure of a game's narrative, developers can create experiences that explore and enhance human virtues, resilience, and pragmatic consciousness. Developers can perceive and treat negative emotions in gaming as the Stoics did - as interpretive responses to external stimuli. Through this re-orientation of player emotions, game designers can construct influential narratives that uplift players, enhancing both their gameplay experience and their personal growth.

11.2. Player Autonomy and Stoicism

A crucial aspect of game design that Stoicism can enhance is player autonomy or decision-making freedom. Emphasizing principles like discretion, self-control, and resilience can shape players' decisions throughout their gaming journey. By integrating Stoic virtues into the consequence system in games, developers can offer players fulfilling challenges as well as profound life wisdom.

11.3. Emphasizing On Mindful Gameplay

Another burgeoning concept in game design is mindful gaming. Infusing principles of stoicism can help developers create experiences that encourage concentration, positive engagement, and self-reflection. This approach can help reshape the gaming industry as one that contributes positively to mental health and emotional resilience.

Despite the promise and prospects that Stoic game design holds, we must also acknowledge the hurdles that might arise on this odyssey.

11.4. Navigating The Challenge of Complexity

Translating a complex philosophy such as Stoicism into the design of a game is a formidable task. Trying to encapsulate its wide breadth of wisdom and teachings within the virtual realms of gaming might also risk oversimplification or misrepresentation. This challenge calls for an in-depth understanding of Stoic philosophy and a creative methodology for its successful implementation.

11.5. Balancing Entertainment and Enlightenment

While leveraging the wisdom of Stoicism can provide profound experiences, maintaining the 'fun' element of games is vital. It will require a fine balance to ensure that games don't become too didactic or monotonous, both of which can deter players. Thus, subtly incorporating elements of Stoic wisdom to enrich rather than override can be a tricky but vital strategy.

11.6. Counteracting Misinterpretations

Since Stoicism is based on individual perspectives towards life, the same principles can lead to diverse interpretations by different players. It is crucial to handle this aspect mindfully to prevent any misinterpretations or dilution of Stoic wisdom.

This exploration into the future of Stoic game design is an acknowledgement of the fertile ground that Stoic philosophy offers to game design, holding the promise of a multitude of successful implementations. These insights are a stepping stone in this rich and exciting journey towards creating gaming experiences that are not just immersive and entertaining, but also transformative and illuminative. In the face of the unforeseen challenges and prospects, Stoic game design is an exciting frontier filled with untapped potential for sincere, thoughtful game creators and players alike.

* 9 7 9 8 8 5 6 0 8 8 7 8 5 *